Y0-ABU-173

MAP AND GUIDE

NATIONAL MUSEUM OF THE AMERICAN INDIAN
Smithsonian Institution, Washington, D.C.

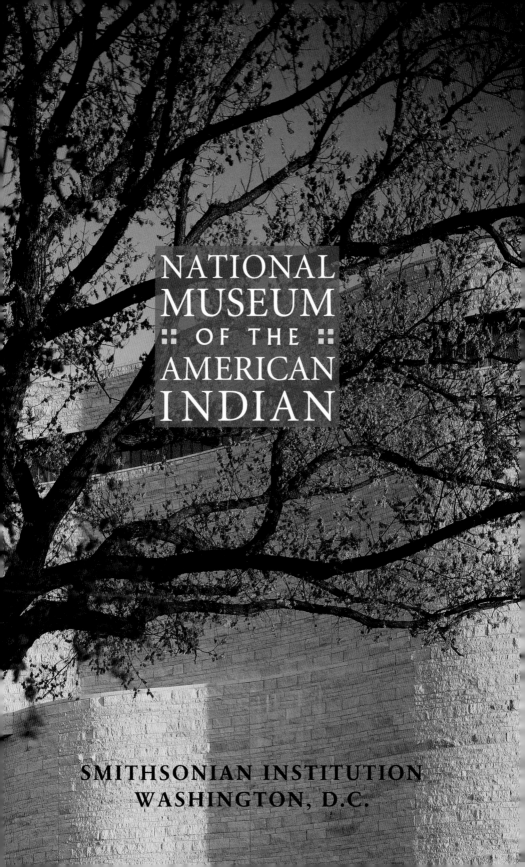

NATIONAL MUSEUM :: OF THE :: AMERICAN INDIAN

SMITHSONIAN INSTITUTION
WASHINGTON, D.C.

Copyright 2012. Illustrations and text, copyright 2012 NMAI, Smithsonian Institution, unless otherwise noted.

All rights reserved. No part of this book may be reproduced in any form without the prior permission of the Smithsonian Institution and the National Museum of the American Indian.

Library of Congress
Cataloging-in-Publication Data

National Museum of the American Indian (U.S.)
  National Museum of the American Indian : map and guide.
    p. cm.
  ISBN 978-1-933565-18-7 (alk. paper)
  1. National Museum of the American Indian (U.S.)—Guidebooks. I. Title.
  E76.86.W182N374 2012
  305.8970074'753--dc23
            2011052311

Associate Director for Museum Programs:
Tim Johnson (Mohawk)

Publications Manager:
Tanya Thrasher (Cherokee)

Editors: Christine T. Gordon, Alexandra Harris, Amy Pickworth

Designer: Steve Bell

Architectural Consultant:
Duane Blue Spruce
(Laguna/Ohkay Owingeh)

Photo Editor and Design Assistant:
Guarina Lopez-Davis (Pascua Yaqui)

Editorial Assistance:
Arwen Nutall (Four Winds Band of Cherokee)
Rachel Beth Sayet (Mohegan)

Special thanks to Cynthia Frankenburg, Ann Kawasaki, Hayes Lavis, Colleen Schreier, Holly Stewart, Thomas Sweeney (Citizen Potawatomi), Leslie Wheelock (Onieda), Randel Wilson, and our beloved late colleagues Helen Scheirbeck (Lumbee) and Lou Stancari.

Printed and bound in China by RR Donnelley

The National Museum of the American Indian, Smithsonian Institution, is dedicated to working in collaboration with the indigenous peoples of the Americas to foster and protect Native cultures throughout the Western Hemisphere. The museum's publishing program seeks to augment awareness of Native American beliefs and lifeways, and to educate the public about the history and significance of Native cultures.

www.AmericanIndian.si.edu

CONTENTS

welcome to
A NATIVE PLACE

WHEN THIS BOOK was first published, the interior of the National Museum of the American Indian on the National Mall was being finished. Art installations were underway. The landscape was being planted. The difference between then and now is more than a matter of months and years—it's the difference between blueprints and reality.

Since 2004, we have mounted groundbreaking and sometimes controversial exhibitions and presented thousands of programs by performers from across the Americas. We've expanded our ties with communities and cultural organizations and launched important scholarship and contemporary art initiatives. We're bringing in new permanent exhibitions. Outside, the museum landscape continues to draw a range of wildlife. The four habitats now feature commissioned artwork, and visitors can find informative labels about the plants and animals found there, with additional details available in our landscape audio guide.

My tenure as director of the NMAI began in 2007, and I am indebted to those who envisioned this museum and saw it through its first few years in service. I am also profoundly grateful to our current staff, and to the more than 12 million visitors who have walked through our doors.

This is no ordinary building. Designed with great care, it resonates with meaning. In the original foreword to the book, the NMAI's founding director, W. Richard West, Jr., spoke of his fervent hope that the museum would be a place of enlightenment. Several years later, as we publish this revised edition and are entering a new era in the life of the museum, I couldn't agree more. Welcome to the NMAI, or welcome back. We're glad you're here.

—Kevin Gover (Pawnee), Director,
National Museum of the American Indian

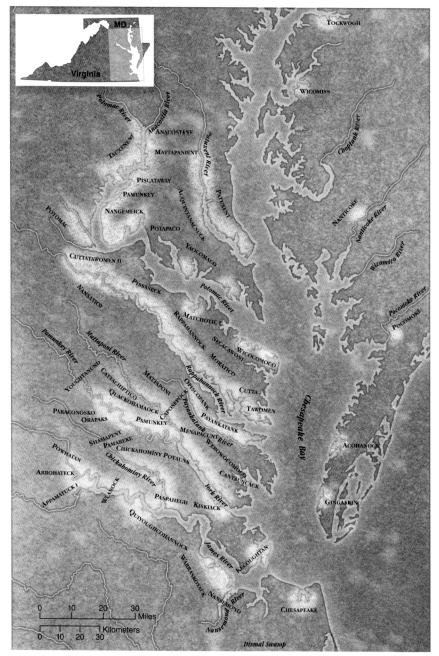

Native Communities in the Chesapeake Bay Area, ca. 1610

Many dozens of different tribal communities were located along the banks of the Chesapeake Bay and its tributaries at the time that Europeans first arrived in this area, in the late 16th century. The yellow highlights suggest where the populations were most concentrated, and the larger communities are labeled. During the decades that followed their first contact with Europeans, these original populations were considerably diminished by war, disease, and land seizures.

THE CHESAPEAKE BAY WATERSHED

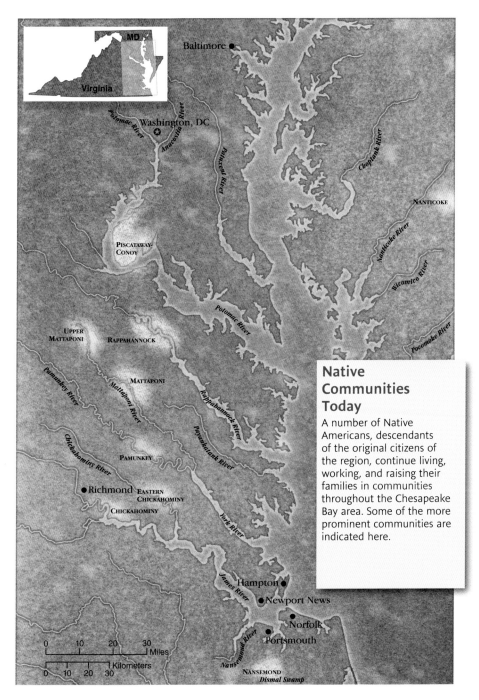

Native Communities Today

A number of Native Americans, descendants of the original citizens of the region, continue living, working, and raising their families in communities throughout the Chesapeake Bay area. Some of the more prominent communities are indicated here.

RETURN TO A NATIVE PLACE

INDIGENOUS PEOPLES OF THE CHESAPEAKE

THE DEEP REALITY UNDERLYING THE ENTIRE WESTERN HEMISPHERE is that this is a Native place. Washington, D.C., is a Native place, as is the Potomac River which embraces its lands.

For thousands of years, indigenous peoples have made their homes along the Potomac and other river tributaries to the Chesapeake Bay. Archeologists estimate that we have occupied the area for about 11,000 years, but Native peoples believe that the Creator brought us here long before that, in mythic time. We have strong connections both to the land and the water. In the Native conception, rivers are not boundaries that divide people; rather, they bring us together.

The tribes of the Chesapeake Bay region's coastal plain are Algonquian, all part of the same language family. At the time of the European settlement at Jamestown in 1607, many Native peoples were organized into thriving chiefdoms—affiliations of numerous tribes to one central chief's town, which served as a center of government. Within 100 years after English occupation, our populations were decimated by war, disease, and land seizures.

"The earth is still here. The water is still here. And we are still here."

—Chief Billy Redwing Tayac (Piscataway)
pictured with his son Mark, at left,
NMAI Groundbreaking Ceremony, 1999

But some of our peoples, through determination and sacrifice, survived over the centuries and have been quite active since the 19th century. Today there are contemporary Powhatan, Piscataway, and Nanticoke communities finding new ways to fit ancestral identities into a modern world. There are many throughout the Chesapeake region who seek to connect to their indigenous roots again. Along with the land and the water, we are still here. This ancient Native place has been reclaimed.

—Gabrielle Tayac (Piscataway)

Children playing "bear in the ring," Nanticoke, Delaware. Boy facing camera is Roosevelt Perkins. Photo by Frank G. Speck, ca. 1911–14. N01304

11

INDIANS IN D.C. TODAY

CHANGE IS INHERENT in the nature of any community, Native or not. Children are born and grow up and have children of their own; people die or move away from the community or decide to join it. A number of American Indian tribes, descendants of those peoples who inhabited the Washington area at the time of first contact with Europeans, still live today in Maryland, Virginia, and Delaware, while a growing urban Indian community, the result of a migration of individuals from many different tribes, has sprung up in Washington in the last several decades.

More than most places, Washington is a town largely populated by people who were not born here. Its American Indian community is fairly well educated, well employed, and stable, with many individuals drawn here by work for federal agencies or non-profit organizations. Famous for building many of New York's skyscrapers, Mohawk iron workers continued that tradition in D.C. by helping construct the Washington Metrorail system. Native Americans currently hold the honor of serving in the U.S. military in larger numbers, per capita, than any other group. Many Native people moved to Washington specifically to work for the National Museum of the American Indian.

The Civil Rights Movement had an important effect on American Indians and, in the mid-1960s, tribal people from communities out West began to come to Washington as part of protest groups. Other groups came not to protest but to lobby Congress or press various federal agencies for better treatment of Native people.

More recently, hundreds of young American Indian college students have come to Washington every summer as interns, their numbers increasing each year. While in D.C. they work and study, receiving school credit for their efforts. The interns often join together to celebrate the end of their sojourn in Washington with a powwow at American University, although for some, this will be the beginning of their lives as members of the Indian community in D.C.

—Mitchell Bush (Onondaga), President Emeritus, American Indian Society

Modern Natives/Personal Regalia is a photography-based project funded by the D.C. Commission on the Arts and Humanities in 2010. Through photographs and interviews, *Personal Regalia* depicts the lives of contemporary Native Americans living in Washington, D.C. (Top row) Jill Norwood (Tolowa/Yurok/Karuk), Wren Woodis (Navajo/Jicarilla Apache); (center row) Taylor Woodis (Navajo/Jicarilla Apache), Melissa Scalph (Adopted Hawaiian), Wilbur Woodis (Navajo); (bottom row) Emil Her Many Horses (Oglala Lakota), Renée Gokey and Eugene Rhyu (Eastern Shawnee/Sac and Fox), Pamela Woodis (Jicarilla Apache), Eric Hall (Tlingit/Haida).

HISTORY OF THE NATIONAL MUSEUM OF THE AMERICAN INDIAN COLLECTION

FOR ONE MAN, WHAT BEGAN AS A SIMPLE INTEREST IN "ABORIGINAL ART" developed into a near obsession, eventually resulting in the most extensive collection of Native American art and artifacts in the world. George Gustav Heye (1874–1957) was born in New York City to a wealthy family and graduated from Columbia College in 1896 with a degree in electrical engineering. While on a work assignment in Arizona, Heye (pronounced HIGH) acquired a Navajo deerskin shirt, sparking his lifelong passion for collecting Indian artifacts.

Heye began traveling the country, buying up Native American objects from tribes, villages, and dealers, and shipping them back to New York. His interest was not limited to the rarest or most significant pieces from a given tribe; rather, Heye would buy entire households full of objects, from the major to the mundane. Heye also traveled to Europe and purchased early examples of Native American art from other collections.

Heye did not confine his collecting to objects. Early on, he recognized that photographs would be an important way to document the cultures of Native peoples, and sought out photographers who had traveled throughout North and South America capturing Native lifeways. Heye sponsored expeditions to the farthest reaches of the Western Hemisphere, sometimes traveling with the anthropologists and photographers he had hired. He bought not only prints but lantern slides and even glass-plate negatives, amassing a collection that today has grown to 125,000 photographic images.

Heye's ever-expanding bounty was initially stored in his Madison Avenue apartment and later in a rented space. In 1916 he estab-

Kiowa shield and cover. Collected in 1910. Rawhide, buckskin, crow and sparrow hawk feathers, red wool trade cloth, horsehairs, pigment, 87.7 x 62.5 x 11.5 cm. 2/8376

George Gustav Heye and his wife, Thea, with a Zuni delegation
in front of the 155th Street museum, ca. 1923. N08130

lished the Museum of the American Indian, Heye Foundation, and in 1922 opened a new building in Manhattan at 155th Street and Broadway to the public. The Museum of the American Indian offered tourists and New Yorkers alike a rare glimpse into the lives of Native Americans. Eventually, the collection spilled over into a warehouse in the Bronx, known as the Research Branch, where scholars, researchers, and Native people were encouraged to share information about the objects housed there. Heye had personal contact with some of the Native people from whom he collected. In 1938, the Hidatsa of North Dakota gave him the name of Isatsigibis, or "Slim Shin," when he returned a sacred bundle to the elders of the tribe.

Heye served as director of his museum until 1956. In 1989, the Museum of the American Indian became part of the Smithsonian Institution by an act of Congress. In 1994, the museum opened its George Gustav Heye Center, located in the historic Alexander Hamilton U.S. Custom House in lower Manhattan. The museum's vast collections, once stored at the Research Branch, have been relocated to the Cultural Resources Center, a state-of-the-art research facility in Suitland, Maryland, just six miles from the museum on the National Mall.

—Danyelle Means (Oglala Lakota)

A NEW MUSEUM IS BORN

THE SMITHSONIAN
NATIONAL MUSEUM
OF THE AMERICAN INDIAN

IN 1989, CONGRESS PASSED Public Law 101-185, sponsored by Senator (then Congressman) Ben Nighthorse Campbell (Northern Cheyenne) of Colorado and Senator Daniel Inouye of Hawai'i, establishing the National Museum of the American Indian as part of the Smithsonian Institution. The law provided for the transfer of assets of the Heye Foundation and appropriated funds for the construction of facilities at three sites: the Alexander Hamilton U.S. Custom House in New York City, the Cultural Resources Center at Suitland, Maryland, and a new museum on the National Mall in Washington, D.C.

One Hundred First Congress of the United States of America

AT THE FIRST SESSION

Begun and held at the City of Washington on Tuesday, the third day of January, one thousand nine hundred and eighty-nine

An Act

To establish the National Museum of the American Indian within the Smithsonian Institution, and for other purposes.

Be it enacted by the Senate and House of Representatives of the United States of America in Congress assembled,

SECTION 1. SHORT TITLE.

This Act may be cited as the "National Museum of the American Indian Act".

SEC. 2. FINDINGS.

The Congress finds that—
(1) there is no national museum devoted exclusively to the history and art of cultures indigenous to the Americas;
(2) although the Smithsonian Institution sponsors extensive Native American programs, none of its 19 museums, galleries, and major research facilities is devoted exclusively to Native American history and art;
(3) the Heye Museum in New York, New York, one of the largest Native American collections in the world, has more than 1,000,000 art objects and artifacts and a library of 40,000 volumes relating to the archaeology, ethnology, and history of Native American peoples;
(4) the Heye Museum is housed in facilities with a total area of 90,000 square feet, but requires a minimum of 400,000 square feet for exhibition, storage, and scholarly research;
(5) the bringing together of the Heye Museum collection and the Native American collection of the Smithsonian Institution would—
　(A) create a national institution with unrivaled capability for exhibition and research;
　(B) give all Americans the opportunity to learn of the cultural legacy, historic grandeur, and contemporary culture of Native Americans;
　(C) provide facilities for scholarly meetings and the performing arts;
　(D) make available curatorial and other learning opportunities for Indians; and
　(E) make possible traveling exhibitions to communities throughout the Nation;
(6) by order of the Surgeon General of the Army, approximately 4,000 Indian human remains from battlefields and burial sites were sent to the Army Medical Museum and were later transferred to the Smithsonian Institution;
(7) through archaeological excavations, individual donations, and museum donations, the Smithsonian Institution has acquired approximately 14,000 additional Indian human remains;
(8) the human remains referred to in paragraphs (6) and (7) have long been a matter of concern for many Indian tribes,

CONSULTATIONS AND PREPARATION

THE ESTABLISHMENT OF THE NMAI within the Smithsonian Institution ended years of uncertainty and debate among Indians, museums, and the general public about the future of one of the world's great collections of objects and archival materials related to the Native peoples of the Western Hemisphere. It also opened a period of planning as to what the mission, programs, and physical spaces of the new museum ought to be, and how it would interact with both its sister institutions and with Native communities throughout the Americas.

Beginning in the early 1990s, the NMAI commenced what would be the first of hundreds of conversations with Indians throughout the Western Hemisphere about how the museum should present the stories and customs of their communities. Through what was and continues to be learned from these close relationships with Native communities, the museum seeks to address and reach beyond misconceptions and stereotypes of Native American cultures and peoples and to illuminate how Native Americans perceive their place—spiritually, historically, and physically—in the universe. These dialogues, which have informed the design of the museum building and the content and philosophy of the museum's exhibitions and public programs, enable visitors to understand what it means to be welcomed to a Native place.

Irene Bá Pop (Q'eqchi Maya) demonstrates Maya weaving to Kalley Keams (Navajo) as she begins a *huipil*.

Scholars and Native community members collaborate to prepare for the *Infinity of Nations* exhibition, 2007. (Left to right) Robert Davidson, Haida artist; Nora Dauenhauer, Tlingit scholar; and Cécile R. Ganteaume, NMAI associate curator.

The Yagán honored the departure of the stone they selected for the southern marker from Chile with a community picnic and farewell.

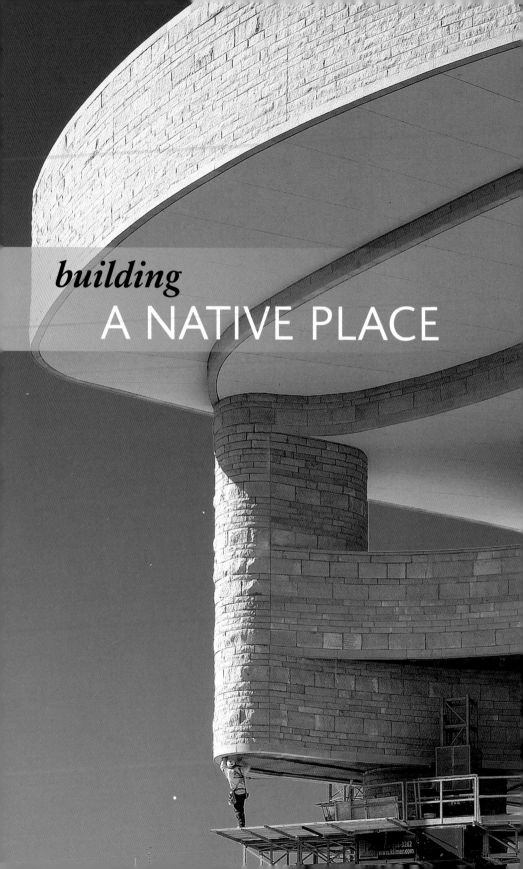

building
A NATIVE PLACE

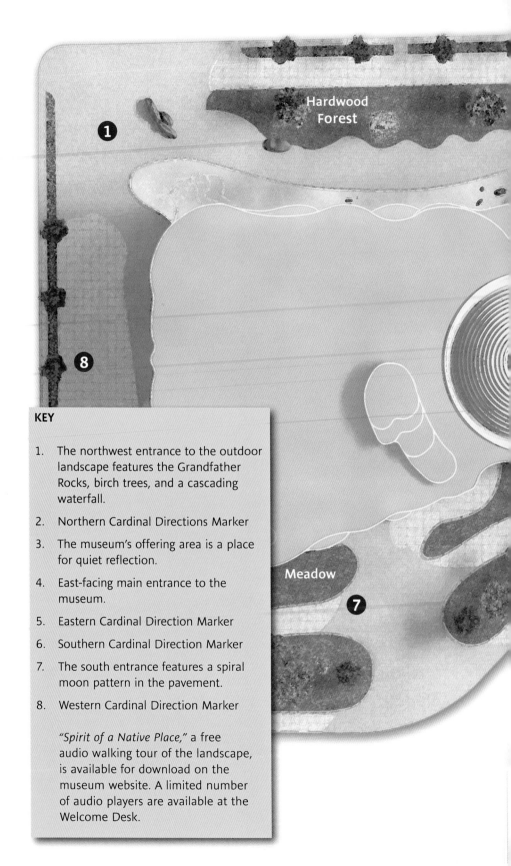

Hardwood Forest

Meadow

KEY

1. The northwest entrance to the outdoor landscape features the Grandfather Rocks, birch trees, and a cascading waterfall.

2. Northern Cardinal Directions Marker

3. The museum's offering area is a place for quiet reflection.

4. East-facing main entrance to the museum.

5. Eastern Cardinal Direction Marker

6. Southern Cardinal Direction Marker

7. The south entrance features a spiral moon pattern in the pavement.

8. Western Cardinal Direction Marker

"Spirit of a Native Place," a free audio walking tour of the landscape, is available for download on the museum website. A limited number of audio players are available at the Welcome Desk.

Wetlands

3

4

5

roplands

North

U.S. Capitol

West

National Mall

NMAI

East

South

THE NATIVE LANDSCAPE

"Until you realize that you are the flowers and the meadows and the forest and the mountains around you, you will not know who you are."

—Indigenous elder, as quoted by Donna House
(Navajo/Oneida, NMAI consultant)

NATIVE PEOPLE believe that the earth remembers the experiences of past generations. The National Museum of the American Indian recognizes the importance of indigenous peoples' connection to the land; the grounds surrounding the building are considered an extension of the building and a vital part of the museum as a whole. By recalling the natural environment that existed prior to European contact, the museum's landscape design embodies a theme that runs central to the NMAI—that of returning to a Native place.

More than 33,000 plants of 150 species can be found throughout the landscape and its four habitats.

Forest

A forest environment runs along the northern edge of the museum site. Forests have provided indigenous cultures with important materials for shelter, firewood, medicines, and other purposes. More than 25 tree species are included in the forest, including red maple, staghorn sumac, and white oak.

Always Becoming sculptures by artist Nora Naranjo-Morse (Santa Clara Pueblo), 2007.

Water lilies and pickerelweed in the museum's wetlands.

Wetlands

Culturally important to many tribes, wetlands are rich, biologically diverse environments. Wild rice, morel mushrooms, marsh marigolds, cardinal flowers, and silky willows are among the species planted at the eastern end of the museum site.

Zuni waffle garden in winter.

Traditional Croplands

This area on the south side of the building features medicinal plants and some of the food crops that Native peoples have given to the world, including the "Three Sisters"—corn, beans, and squash. The plants in this area are cultivated using traditional Native agricultural techniques.

Meadow

Buttercups, fall panic grass, and sunflowers are among the plants featured in the meadow, located southwest of the museum building.

Butterfly on swamp milkweed.

Grandfather Rocks

More than 40 large uncarved rocks and boulders, called Grandfather Rocks because they are the elders of the land-scape, welcome visitors to the museum grounds and serve as reminders of the longevity of Native peoples' relation-ships to the environment. The Grandfather Rocks, hewn by wind and water for millions of years, were selected from a quarry area in Alma, Canada. The boulders were blessed in a special ceremony by the Montagnais First Nations group prior to their relocation, to ensure that they would have a safe journey and carry the message and cultural memory of past generations to future generations. Upon arriving in Washington, the boulders were welcomed to their new home in a blessing by a member of the Monacan Nation of Virginia.

Cardinal Direction Markers

A subtle yet significant design concept, the Cardinal Direction Markers are four special stones placed in the museum grounds along the north-south and east-west axes. These axes intersect inside the building at the center of the Potomac area of the museum, linking the four directions and their markers to the circle of red Seneca sandstone that marks the figurative heart of the museum. The mark-ers also serve as metaphors for the indigenous peoples of the Americas. The stones have traveled from the far reaches of the hemisphere in collaboration with their Native source communities: Hawai'i (western marker stone); Northwest Territories, Canada (northern stone); Great Falls, Maryland (eastern stone); and Punto Arenas, Chile (southern stone).

The northern cardinal direction marker in the museum's woodlands

23

"The building must have a language of its own, a language that speaks for the aboriginal peoples of the Americas, a language that wraps the visitor in a different paradigm of perception."
—NMAI document, 1996

SHAPED BY WIND AND WATER

FOR MANY NATIVE PEOPLES of the Western Hemisphere, significant and sometimes spiritual places are often part of the natural world, such as rock formations, lakes, rivers, forests, canyons, and mountains. These kinds of natural settings—as well as the stone and masonry work of Chaco Canyon, Machu Picchu, and other Native sites—inspired NMAI building designers to create a museum and landscape that welcome visitors to a distinctly Native place, one that reflects and honors the organic and emphasizes that people are part of a larger natural world.

Eroded sandstone, Vermillion Wilderness, Arizona

NATIVE DESIGN ELEMENTS

The stonework at the museum's south entrance symbolizes the 18.6-year lunar standstill cycle.

"As tribal people of the Western Hemisphere, we are wonderfully diverse yet essentially similar. We honor the exquisite variety of each other's lifeways, yet recognize that we have some common principles that are essential in the representation and interpretation of our respective ways of being. The museum's designs and operations will be guided by these principles."

—Rina Swentzell (Tewa/Santa Clara Pueblo), Preamble to *The Way of the People*, 1993

THE DESIGN TEAM WAS ASKED TO CREATE A PALETTE OF COLORS, materials, symbols, and forms that would imbue the building and site with a Native sensibility. Themes emerged, including abstractions of nature and astronomy. For example, the paving pattern for the Welcome Plaza area outside the east entrance plots the configuration of the planets on November 28, 1989, the date that federal legislation was introduced to create the museum. The center of the plaza is the polestar, Polaris. The museum's south-entry plaza records lunar events, and, inside the building, the Potomac celebrates the sun. The angles of solstices and equinoxes are mapped on the Potomac's floor, and a light spectrum is cast above by the sun shining through prisms set into the south-facing wall.

Copper screen wall, Potomac.

During the development of the NMAI building, we held close a rich array of images and abstracted Native places. The color palette is heavily inspired by the natural world and the NMAI collection. The cafe drapes itself in the colors and textures of corn, beans, squash, and fish. Objects from the collection lend their hues to areas throughout the building.

Shell inlay, museum stores.

I brought my own experiences to the project, and the project in turn has changed me. I feel greatly honored to have been part of this adventure.

—Ramona Sakiestewa (Hopi),
Design Consultant

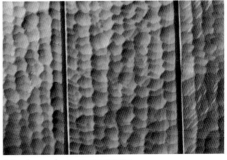

Adzed wood, museum stores.

27

1
LEVEL

Real-life Quechua healer Honorato Ninantay portraying Don Santos Condori in NMAI's signature film, *A Thousand Roads*.

- **Welcome Desk** (visitor information)

- **Potomac Atrium** (Highlights Tours begin here)

- **Elevators to Levels 2, 3, and 4**

- **Mitsitam Native Foods Cafe**

- **Group Orientation Room**

- **Rasmuson Theater**

- **Group Entrance**

Stairs

Group Orientation Room

Group and South Entrance →

Stairs

Elevators

Native Americas Interactive Map

Potomac Atrium

Welcome Desk

East Entrance

For Life in All Directions, (detail) by Roxanne Swentzell (Santa Clara, b. 1962), 2004. New Mexico. Bronze, ceramic. 26/4546

Mitsitam Native Foods Cafe serves food inspired by Native dishes.

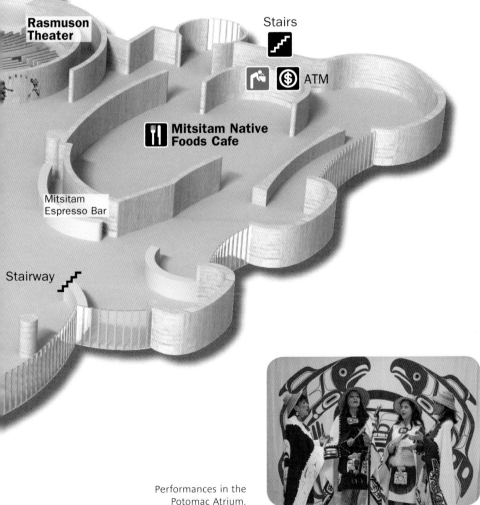

Rasmuson Theater

Stairs

ATM

Mitsitam Native Foods Cafe

Mitsitam Espresso Bar

Stairway

Performances in the Potomac Atrium.

public programs
ENTERING THE MUSEUM

THE POTOMAC

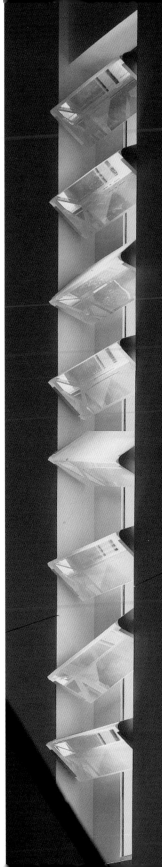

RIVERS OFTEN SERVE as points of reference and connection for the people who live near them. This idea was a major influence in building a distinctly Native public space on the National Mall in Washington, D.C., an area that lies between two rivers, the Potomac and the Anacostia. Early in the consultations with Native communities, it became clear that the museum required a large central gathering place that needed to be more than a simple rotunda; this space should refer to the organization of the Native world and be a place of connection to contemporary Native activity. Further, it should honor the Native people from the Washington area.

The resulting space, the Potomac (from the Iroquoian/Delaware/Powhatan word meaning "where the goods are brought in"), is the point of entry for most visitors and a venue for a variety of performances and other cultural exchanges. Soaring 120 feet to the top of the dome and spanning more than 100 feet in diameter, the Potomac is the very heart of the museum building, the sun of its universe, and celestial references abound.

Prisms in the south-facing wall of the museum. This design feature, created by New York artist Charles Ross, reminds visitors of the location and path of the sun.

(Clockwise, from top left) Tribal flags span the Potomac over a performance during Native American Heritage Month; The Git-hoan Native Dance Group performs for the unveiling of *Eagle and Young Chief*, a totem pole created by Tsimshian carvers David Boxley and his son David Robert Boxley; Dominic Arquero (Cochito Pueblo) demonstrates gourd carving and painting during the Living Earth Festival; performance artist Thirza Defoe (Ojibwa/Oneida Nation of Wisconsin) explores the roots of identity through performance.

Facing east to greet the morning sun, the main doors opening into the Potomac are etched with sun symbols from Native cultures. An oculus in the dome five stories above the space provides views of the sky. The recessed, divided circle in the floor of the Potomac Rotunda honors the four cardinal directions. At its center, representing the heart of the museum, is a smaller circle of red Seneca sandstone. The sandstone was sourced locally, near Seneca Creek, Maryland. Much of early Washington, D.C., architecture was crafted from this stone, and it is the same stone used on the Smithsonian's main building, the "Castle." The axes of the solstices and equinoxes are mapped on the floor with rings of red and black granite. Eight large glass prisms glitter from a window in the south wall, each sited to the sun for a particular time of day and season.

A wall of woven copper bands encircles the Potomac. Textured with a solar pattern, this dramatic screen evokes the weaving traditions of Native basketry and textiles. Elevators leading to the exhibition areas feature different bird motifs that refer to flight and the cardinal directions.

—Linda R. Martin (Navajo)

WELCOME TO A NATIVE PLACE

THE POTOMAC, YOUR POINT OF ENTRY INTO THE MUSEUM, is often a gathering place for music, dance, cultural events and tours.

Large thematic ideas that introduce the visitor to Native communities of the Western hemisphere, from the present day to historic past, are also on view in the museum's first floor exhibition spaces. Here visitors can learn about dance, drama, music, and Native foodways, among other topics.

(Top left) A fancy dancer at the NMAI National Powwow, 2007.

(Top right) Jose Chavez (Pascua Yaqui) preparing for a dance, 1920. Guadalupe, Arizona. Photo by Edward H. Davis. N24392

(Middle left) Clown figure, 2005. Made by Lisa Holt (Cochiti Pueblo, b. 1980), and Harlan Reano (Kewa Pueblo, b. 1978). Pottery, paint, 37 x 15 x 50 cm. 26/5237

(Middle right) Gwich'in (Kutchin) boots, ca. 1970. Arctic Red River, Northwest Territories, Canada. Moose hide, wool felt, cotton cloth, wolverine fur, wool yarn, hide thong, ribbon, thread. Gift of Juliet Ridard, 1997. 25/4557

Darrell L. Norman (Pikuni Blackfeet, b. 1943), *Napi Gives People Life*, 1997. Browning, Montana. Rawhide, wood, glass beads, feathers, wool cloth, cotton cloth, brass bells, paint. Gift of R. E. Mansfield. 26/4321

PUBLIC PROGRAMS

Chili harvesting during the Living Earth Festival, 2010.

The International Company of Scissor Dancers Hermanos Chávez dance at the Power of Chocolate Festival.

IN SHOWCASING THE HISTORY and cultural expression of indigenous peoples of the Americas, including Native Hawaiians, NMAI public programs present a variety of engaging educational activities. Native presentations, stage plays, dance and music performances, demonstrations, lectures, film screenings, symposia, and seminars are held in indoor and outdoor spaces, including the Rasmuson Theater, the Outdoor Amphitheater, and the Potomac area, as well as in classrooms and the Conference Center. The museum's imagiNATIONS Activity Center offers a family-friendly opportunity to explore Native cultures and the NMAI's collections through interactive games, discovery boxes, make-and-take projects, and other fun hands-on activities.

NMAI's Film and Video Center, located in Washington, D.C., and New York, is dedicated to presenting and disseminating information about the work of Native Americans in media. The center hosts film festivals, screenings, and symposia, and maintains a website, **www.nativenetworks.si.edu**, that provides news, calendar listings, and other resources.

—Linda R. Martin (Navajo)

The NMAI's website, **www.AmericanIndian.si.edu**, lists details about exhibitions and events, offers access to teacher materials and resources, and gives information about internship and employment opportunities for students and professionals.

The website also provides information on ordering a variety of books and recordings produced by the NMAI's publications office, including award-winning exhibition-related, special-interest, and children's book titles.

RASMUSON THEATER

Santee Smith (Mohawk) premieres her work *Kahaiwi—She Carries.*

Children's chamber opera performance of *El conejo y el coyote; The Rabbit and the Coyote* by Victor Rasgado (Zapotec).

Poet and musician Joy Harjo (Mvskoke/Creek) performs during the NMAI's Native Writers Series.

THE NATIONAL MUSEUM OF THE AMERICAN INDIAN is filled with visual metaphors that ground the building in the Native world. From the initial concept to its final touches, the theater design was inspired by the metaphor of a perfect storytelling venue: a clearing in the woods under a bright night sky.

Native stories are often told in winter or at night, and visual references to this setting include the moon, the texture of ice, colors used by the Inupiaq people of Alaska, and Raven, a trickster character often found in American Indian stories. Vertical wood paneling surrounds the 322-seat circular theater, evoking a dense hardwood forest, and above, a dark blue ceiling twinkles with constellations. Cast-glass sconces along the back wall recall the phases of the moon. This gathering place brings visitors close to Native performers by incorporating a unique lateral aisle that allows performers to move from the stage through the audience in full circle, consistent with many Native dances. Equipped with multi-media projection systems, language-translation systems, and superb acoustic qualities, the theater hosts a diverse program of Native musicians, theater companies, dancers, film festivals, and storytellers.

The vertical wood paneling and dark blue ceiling in the NMAI's Rasmuson Theater evoke a clearing in the woods under a bright night sky.

A Thousand Roads, the museum's signature film, is screened daily and follows a day in the life of four contemporary Native Americans.

Shakespeare's *Macbeth*, translated into the Tlingit language and presented by Perseverance Theatre of Juneau, Alaska.

WILD RICE SALAD

In this salad, the cooked rice is blended with pine nuts, pumpkin seeds, and dried cranberries and served on a bed of watercress.

Serves 4 to 6

Apple Cider Vinaigrette
6 tablespoons apple cider vinegar
¼ cup honey
¾ cup canola oil
Salt and freshly ground pepper to taste

Salad
6 cups homemade vegetable stock or canned low-sodium chicken broth
1½ cups wild rice
1 carrot, peeled and cut into 2-inch matchsticks
3 tablespoons dried cranberries
1 plum (Roma) tomato, finely diced
4 to 5 scallions, including some green parts, finely chopped
½ cup pine nuts, toasted and cooled
¼ cup unsalted raw pumpkin seeds, toasted and cooled
3 bunches watercress, stemmed

For the vinaigrette: In a small bowl, combine all the ingredients and whisk to blend. Cover and refrigerate for at least 1 hour, or up to 10 days.

For the salad: In a large saucepan, combine the stock and wild rice. Bring to a boil, then reduce the heat to a simmer. Cover and cook until tender, 45 to 55 minutes. Spread the rice on a baking sheet and let cool. Scrape the rice into a large bowl and

Wild rice salad, from *The Mitsitam Cafe Cookbook: Recipes from the National Museum of the American Indian* by Richard Hetzler. Published by the National Museum of the American Indian in association with Fulcrum Publishing. © 2010 Smithsonian Institution.

add the carrot, dried cranberries, tomato, scallions, pine nuts, and pumpkin seeds. Toss to mix. Add ½ cup vinaigrette and toss to coat. Cover and refrigerate for at least 1 hour. Salad may be served chilled or brought up to room temperature. To serve, divide the watercress among salad plates and top with the wild rice salad.

Note: To toast the pine nuts and pumpkin seeds, preheat the oven to 350 degrees F. Spread the nuts and seeds on a rimmed baking sheet and toast until lightly browned and fragrant, about 8 minutes. Pour into a bowl and let cool.

(Opposite, top) Cedar-planked fire-roasted salmon; (middle) ingredients for pork pibil and beef adobo tacos; (bottom) cranberry crumble.

MITSITAM (mit-seh-TOM) means "let's eat" in the Piscataway and Delaware language. The Zagat-rated Mitsitam Cafe, located on the museum's ground level, offers meals and snacks based on the indigenous foods and culinary traditions of the Americas. From a window seat in the soaring two-story dining space you can gaze out on the water feature that winds along the north side of the building. If you're yearning for a delicious coffee drink or lighter fare, the cafe's new Mitsitam Espresso Bar offers an intimate space to relax within view of the Potomac Atrium. The Espresso Bar serves products from Tribal Grounds Coffee, a company owned by members of the Eastern Band of Cherokee that sources organic, fair-trade coffee grown by indigenous farmers. After your meal, be sure to pick up a copy of the award-winning *Mitsitam Cafe Cookbook*, which features 90 easy-to-follow recipes that will allow you to explore Native culinary traditions in your own kitchen.

THREE INAUGURAL GALLERIES
Over the next few years, the NMAI will close
our three main exhibitions, *Our Universes*,
Our Peoples, and *Our Lives*, and introduce
our visitors to new aspects of the indigenous
experience in the Western Hemisphere. From
the Great Inka Road of Peru to the intricate
treaty relationships between Native nations
and the U.S. government, the new exhibitions
will focus on the history and legacy of
complex and sophisticated cultures.

exhibitions
ENTERING THE NATIVE WORLD

4
LEVEL

- **Lelawi Theater**
- ***Our Universes*** **Exhibition**
- ***Our Peoples*** **Exhibition**
- ***Window on Collections*** **Exhibition**
- **Patrons' Lounge**
- **Conference Center (Rooms 4018/4019)**

LELAWI THEATER
(your visit begins here)

View the film *Who We Are* in the Lelawi Theater.

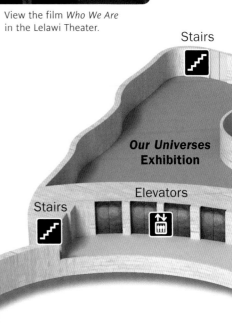

Stairs

Our Universes Exhibition

Elevators

Stairs

Stair

Stairs

Patrons' Lounge

Objects that depict the stars, sun, and moon are among the works displayed in the *Our Universes* exhibition.

The Wall of Gold in the *Our Peoples* exhibition features more than 400 gold objects, most of them created before 1490.

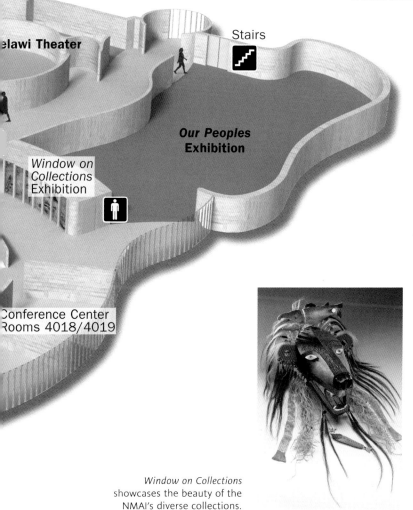

elawi Theater

Stairs

Our Peoples Exhibition

Window on Collections Exhibition

Conference Center Rooms 4018/4019

Window on Collections showcases the beauty of the NMAI's diverse collections.

Inupiat whaling crew watching for bowhead whales. Barrow, Alaska.

Pipemaker Travis Erickson (Sisseton Wahpeton Sioux) in his studio. Pipestone, Minnesota.

Teotihuacán, Mexico.

Hopi, Arizona.

Totem poles at Haida Gwaii, Canada.

LELAWI THEATER

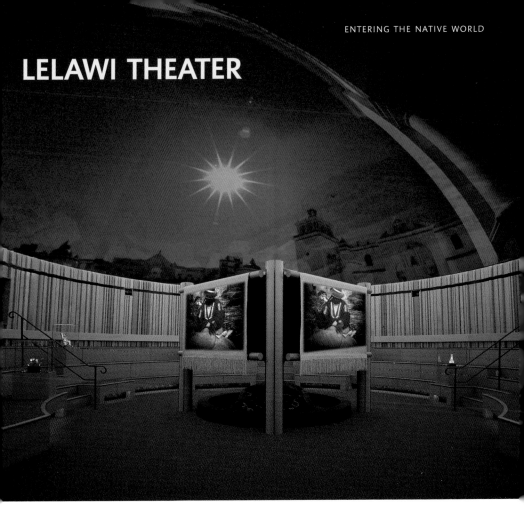

THE 125-SEAT circular Lelawi (leh-LAH-wee) Theater, located adjacent to the *Our Universes* gallery on the fourth level, offers a dazzling multi-media experience designed to prepare museumgoers for the themes and messages they will encounter during a visit to NMAI. *Who We Are*, a 13-minute presentation, immerses viewers in the vibrancy and diversity of contemporary Native life and explores, from a Native perspective, the strength that different communities across the hemisphere derive from their connections to land, community, religion, self-government, and self-expression.

Overhead, images fill the 40-foot dome, transporting viewers to the vast reaches of the Arctic, the cool forests of the Northwest Coast, and the high plateaus of Bolivia. A four-post center structure supports four additional screens, and emerging from the floor is a cast-acrylic "rock" that transforms from a rushing creek to a storyteller's fire. Surrounding visitors are objects from the collection that link to the stories. Among the tribal groups highlighted in the presentation are the Mi'kmaq (east), the Maya and Aymara (south), the Inupiat and Haida (north), and the Hopi, Lakota, and Muscogee Creek (west).

OUR UNIVERSES

TRADITIONAL KNOWLEDGE SHAPES OUR WORLD

The first of NMAI's three main exhibitions, *Our Universes* focuses on Native cosmology—world-views and philosophies relating to the creation and order of the universe—and the spiritual relationship between humankind and the natural world. Organized around one solar year, the exhibition explores annual ceremonies as a window to ancestral Native teachings. Visitors discover how celestial bodies shape the daily lives, and establish the calendars of ceremonies and celebrations, of Native peoples today.

Our Universes explores the Denver March Powwow, the North American Indigenous Games, and the Day of the Dead as seasonal celebrations that bring together different Native peoples. Eight inaugural Native communities—Pueblo of Santa Clara (New Mexico), Anishinaabe (Canada), Lakota (South Dakota), Quechua (Peru), Hupa (California), Q'eq'chi' Maya (Guatemala), Mapuche (Chile), and Yup'ik (Alaska)—share tribal philosophies in distinctive community-curated sections of the exhibition. The structure of each of these galleries reflects each community's own interpretations as to the order of the world.

Comanche Medicine Fan with sun and morning star designs (detail), ca. 1880. Feather, animal hide, wood, cloth, beads, length 68.6 cm. 2/1617

I am Tlingit and my family is of the Eagle Clan on my mother's side. I live in Seattle.

Raven is the one in our culture who brought order to the world. . . . The bases of all my inspiration are [Tlingit] stories and symbols. All of that

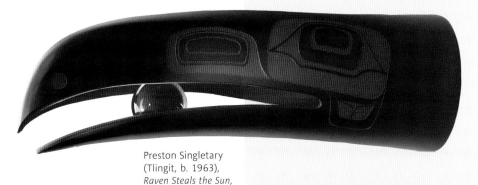

Preston Singletary (Tlingit, b. 1963), *Raven Steals the Sun*, 2003. Blown and sand-carved glass. 26/3273

imagery is brought into the glasswork. I create objects that represent or try to tell something about the culture of the Tlingit people. The stories are a way of passing on knowledge of all aspects of the world, and teachings, and morals. These stories are really important. . . . Time spent listening to these stories and trying to understand the metaphors that are behind them gives you a lot of insight into life.

—From an interview with Preston Singletary, whose commissioned piece *Raven Steals the Sun* is a highlight of the *Our Universes* exhibition

Mapuche *kultrung* (drum) with stick. Wood, leather, horsehair, paint. Chile. 17/5797; Mapuche *makuñ* (poncho), early 20th century. Wool, natural dyes. Chile. 17/6736

OUR PEOPLES
GIVING VOICE TO OUR HISTORIES

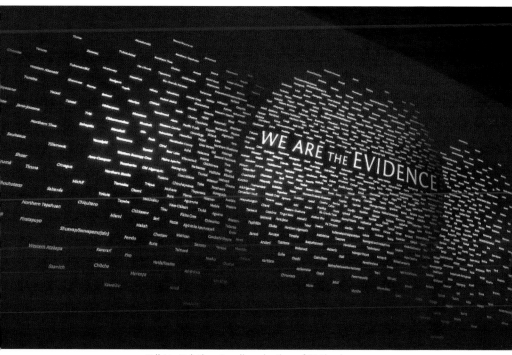

"All My Relations" wall projection of Native languages.

"We are the evidence of this Western Hemisphere."
—Henry Crow Dog (Lakota), 1974

NATIVE PEOPLES, when not left out completely, are often portrayed in textbooks in narrow or inaccurate ways. In *Our Peoples*, American Indians tell their own stories; in this way the exhibition presents new insights into, and different versions of, history. This exhibition encourages viewers to consider history not as a single, definitive, immutable work, but as a collection of subjective tellings by different authors with different points of view. Visitors are invited to question, *What is history and who writes it?* as they look at the last five centuries from the vantage point of eight groups of American Indians. The Blackfeet (Montana), Chiricahua Apache (New Mexico), Kiowa (Oklahoma), Tohono O'odham (Arizona), Eastern Band of Cherokee (North Carolina), Nahua (Mexico), Ka'apor (Brazil), and Wixáritari—sometimes known as Huichol—(Mexico) author their own tribal histories, sharing with visitors a few of the myriad stories that represent American Indian experience.

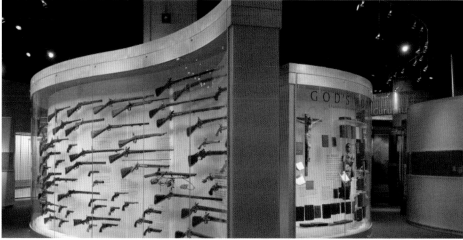

(Top left) Treaties and their legacy, part of "The Storm: Guns, Bibles, and Governments."

(Top right) Blackfeet tobacco cutting board. Wood, brass, tacks. 30 x 30 cm. 22/1807; Blackfeet knife (and case, not shown). 11/7037

(Middle) Firearm and Bible display in "The Storm."

(Bottom) *Eye of the Storm* by artist Edward Poitras (Salteaux/Métis).

OUR PEOPLES
A HISTORY OF RESILIENCE

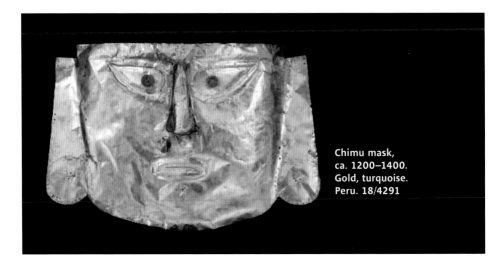

**Chimu mask,
ca. 1200–1400.
Gold, turquoise.
Peru. 18/4291**

POWERFUL FORCES have transformed life in the Americas since 1492. Before Columbus's arrival, tens of millions of Native people made their homes here in deserts, on mountains, in fishing villages, and in crowded cities. They spoke hundreds of different languages and lived complex lives as kings, scientists, farmers, artists, cooks, dreamers, hunters, and students. After Columbus and other explorers arrived, American gold made Spain the richest country in the world, while epidemics of diseases introduced by Europeans raged across the hemisphere for 150 years, claiming as many as nine lives out of ten in some Native communities. Those who lived often found themselves pushed out of the lands their people had inhabited for thousands of years.

The arrival of Europeans in the Western Hemisphere set the stage for the most momentous series of events in recorded human history. It created the world we live in today, reshaping Africa, Europe, and Asia; fueling the rise of capitalism; and changing the clothes humans wore, the food they consumed, and the ideas they exchanged. In struggling for survival in this new world, every Native community experienced loss in unique ways, but nearly all wrestled with the impact of deadly new weaponry, the weakening of traditional religion and ritual by the Christian church, and the dispossession of traditional lands by other governments. But the story of these last five centuries is not entirely about destruction. It is also a story about resilience; the intentional, strategic adoption of tools and customs by Native peoples in order to keep their cultures alive; and how weaponry, the church, and relationships with other governments have been used by Native peoples to ensure their futures.

Oliver Enjady (Mescalero Apache, b. ca. 1953), *Mangas in Trust*, 2006. Mescalero Apache Reservation, New Mexico. Canvas, acrylic paint, wood, 91.2 x 121.6 cm. 26/5822

51

WINDOW ON COLLECTIONS
MANY HANDS, MANY VOICES

(Left) Thomas Jefferson peace medal, 1801. Belonged to Powder Face (Arapaho). Oklahoma. Copper alloy coin, leather, porcupine quills, feathers, metal. 24/1965

Jenny Ann (Chapoose) Taylor (Unitah Ute, b.?), *Nations*, 2002. Glass beads, commercially tanned leather, nylon thread, 58 x 85 cm. 26/5294

MORE THAN 3000 OBJECTS from the museum's collections are presented in the *Window on Collections* exhibit, located on the third and fourth levels of the museum. Housed in glass-fronted cases located on the balconies overlooking the Potomac area, these presentations include peace medals, beadwork objects, and children's games and clothing. Because only a small portion of the museum's collections can be on display at any one time, *Window on Collections* affords visitors a broad spectrum of the NMAI's ancient and historic objects of great beauty.

Window on Collections allows visitors a glimpse at the remarkable breadth and diversity of objects from the NMAI collection and gives insight into Native experiences through these material legacies.

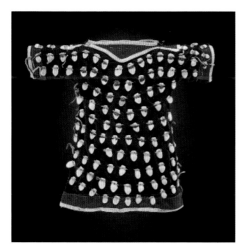

Apsáalooke (Crow) girl's dress, ca. 1915. Montana. Wool and cotton cloth, real and imitation elk teeth, hide, pigments, 47.5 x 53 x 2 cm. 11/7692

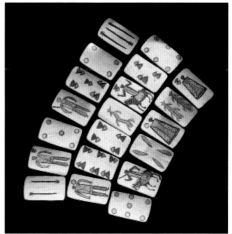

Chiracahua deck of 37 playing cards, ca. 1875–85. Arizona. Rawhide, paint, 9.1 x 5.6 x 1 cm each. 6/4597

3
LEVEL

Faces of Native people in the *Our Lives* Exhibition.

- *Window on Collections*
  Exhibition

- **imagiNATIONS**
  Activity Center

- *Our Lives*
  Exhibition

- **W. Richard West, Jr.**
  Contemporary Arts Gallery

- **Education Classroom**

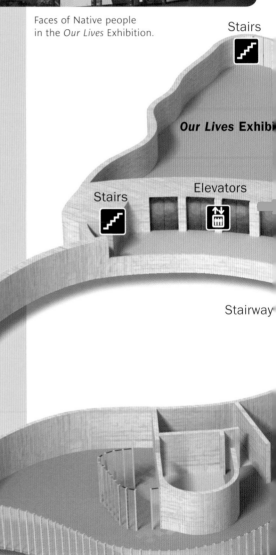

Stairs

Our Lives Exhib►

Stairs

Elevators

Stairway

Cultural interpreter Rachael Cassidy (Cherokee Nation of Oklahoma) leads a school tour.

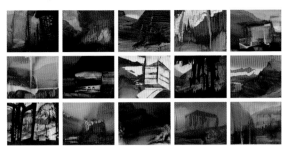

The museum's exhibitions showcase many spectacular pieces of contemporary Native art.

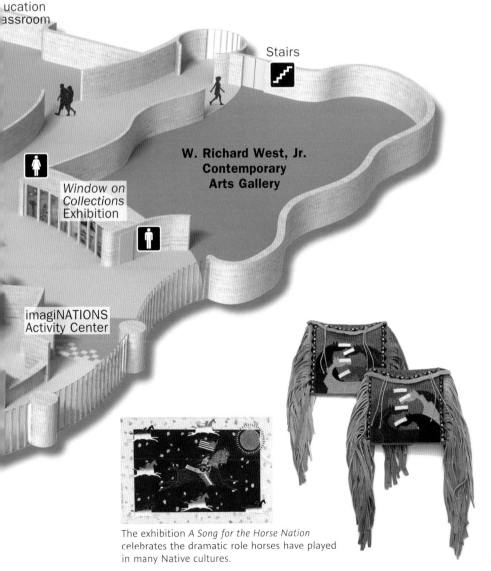

ucation
assroom

Stairs

W. Richard West, Jr.
Contemporary
Arts Gallery

Window on Collections Exhibition

imagiNATIONS
Activity Center

The exhibition *A Song for the Horse Nation* celebrates the dramatic role horses have played in many Native cultures.

OUR LIVES

CONTEMPORARY LIFE AND IDENTITIES

JUST AS THEY DID in 1491, Native Americans today live in a land that is ancient and modern, diverse and always changing. They number in the tens of millions and live in the hemisphere's most remote places and its biggest cities. They fly spacecraft and herd llamas, write software and grow orchids, fight wars and teach chemistry. They trade stock from Park Avenue apartments, drive taxis through Lima's rush hour, and sell shoes in Kentucky strip malls. Modern American Indians are not shadows of their ancestors, but their equals.

—Paul Chaat Smith (Comanche)

In the "Living in a Native Space" portion of *Our Lives,* visitors see how Native people from four different regions of the Americas retain connections with and face challenges to their homelands.

Our Lives examines the identities of Native peoples in the 21st century, and shows how those identities, both individual and communal, are a result of deliberate, often difficult choices made in challenging circumstances. All people are profoundly influenced by the world around them, by their families and communties, the language they speak, the places they live and identify with, and their own self-determination. This exhibition explores each of these forces in modern Native life, as well as another factor unique to contemporary Indian identity: the continuing resonance of imposed legal policies—some of which are five centuries old—regarding who is Indian and what that means. Eight communities contributed their stories to this telling—the Campo Band of Kumeyaay Indians (California), urban Indian community of Chicago (Illinois), Yakama Nation (Washington State), Igloolik (Canada), Kahnawake (Canada), Saint-Laurent Metis (Canada), Kalinago (Carib Territory, Dominica), and the Pamunkey Tribe (Virginia).

TRADITIONAL TECHNIQUES

Gail Tremblay (Onondaga/Mi'kmaq, b. 1945), *Strawberry and Chocolate*, 2000. 16mm film and fullcoat. 25/7273

ALTHOUGH THEY HAVE BEEN MADE by Native people in North America for several thousand years, baskets are, and always have been, contemporary objects, products of the materials, needs, and aesthetic values of the times and cultures in which they were created. Baskets are made for specific purposes, whether for sifting meal, carrying water, storing food, for use in religious ceremonies, or, as is most common in more recent times, for sale. The forms that baskets take, and their shapes and sizes, are typically related to their purpose. As Native people recognized the commercial potential of selling objects to tourists and at other non-Native venues, new styles followed. For example, in the mid 20th century, the traditional technique of splint-plait basketry was employed by Ho-Chunk communities in Wisconsin to create new forms: shallow round baskets, perfect for holding blocks of cheese for sale to local dairy companies. Traditional basket forms have often been adapted to appeal to the contemporary consumer market, resulting in picnic baskets, fruit baskets, market baskets, or decorative baskets, such as the strawberry basket by Eve Point (Mohawk) seen here.

In a twist on traditional forms—and as a wonderful example of the playfulness often seen in contemporary American Indian art—Onondaga/Mi'kmaq artist Gail Tremblay has wed the splint-plait technique to an unusual material: film. This piece is part of a series by Tremblay, an artist and writer who teaches at Evergreen State College in Olympia, Washington. Some of the films woven into baskets in this series are, ironically enough, old cowboy movies.

CONTEMPORARY ART

NMAI'S W. RICHARD WEST, JR. Contemporary Arts Gallery showcases changing exhibitions of Native artworks and underscores the museum's ongoing commitment to contemporary art. The gallery's inaugural exhibition, *Native Modernism: The Art of George Morrison and Allan Houser*, celebrated the work and influence of two lions of the Native art world. Since then, the gallery has featured the works of Fritz Scholder (Luiseño) in *Indian/Not Indian*, Brian Jungen (Dunne-za) in *Strange Comfort*, and significant works by 25 established and emerging artists in *Vantage Point*. The exhibitions in the contemporary arts gallery seek to challenge notions of Native American art and explore people's perspectives on history, culture, and current events.

Fritz Scholder (Luiseño, b. 1937), *The American Indian*, 1970. Oil on linen, 152.4 x 106.7 cm. Indian Arts and Crafts Board Collection, Department of the Interior, at the National Museum of the American Indian, Smithsonian Institution. 26/1056

James Lavadour (Walla Walla), *Blanket*, 2005. Oil on board, 183 x 396 x 5 cm. 26/6079

imagiNATIONS ACTIVITY CENTER

Stunning, life-sized Native architecture (above, left) and a fun and competitive quiz show are two of the many activities visitors will discover in the new imagiNATIONS Activity Center, located on the museum's third level.

VISITORS TO THE INTERACTIVE, family-friendly imagiNATIONS Activity Center can learn about the indigenous cultures of the Americas through replicas of traditional Native homes, discovery boxes, make-and-take projects, and other fun hands-on activities.

For millennia, Native people have used resources from the natural world to meet their needs. The imagiNATIONS Activity Center encourages children to discover how Native people have used their environments to build homes, grow and harvest food, and play games. Find out why snowshoes are so useful, and how Arctic peoples use kayaks. Explore a wetlands ecosystem and discover how plants are used for food and for making baskets. Step inside a full-size tipi and learn about the buffalo. As you journey through the center, celebrate the diversity of hundreds of Native nations by stamping your imagiNATIONS passport with real tribal seals. The center also features a quiz show to test your knowledge, a music room, and a story room where storytellers and artists can demonstrate their talents.

A NATIVE PATH THROUGH D.C.
OTHER POINTS OF INTEREST

The Washington area offers many places of interest for tourists, among them a number that hold special appeal for American Indian visitors and those interested in Native art and culture.

The **U.S. Capitol Building**, just east of the NMAI building, is a great place to start. Statues or busts of Sacagawea (Shoshone), Chief Washakie (Shoshone), Sarah Winnemucca (Paiute), Sequoya (Cherokee), and Po'Pay (Ohkay Owingeh) are on display, as are a number of other Indian-themed paintings, murals, and statuary. Remember, however, that visitors must be part of a scheduled tour to enter the Capitol building. Arrange a visit with your senator or congressperson, phone 202-225-6827, or visit the Capitol's website at www.aoc.gov for more information about joining a scheduled tour.

The **Smithsonian Institution** offers a wealth of resources related to Native culture and artifacts. In particular, the National Museums of Natural History and American History, both located west of NMAI on the National Mall, regularly feature American Indian-related exhibitions. For more information about these museums and other Smithsonian exhibitions and programs, call 202-633-1000, visit the SI website at www.si.edu, or drop by the Smithsonian Information Center in the Castle Building.

The offices of most federal agencies and Indian organizations are not open to visiting tourists. The **Stewart Udall Department of the Interior (DOI) Building** (1849 C Street, NW; 202-298-4743) is a notable exception, although you will need to schedule an appointment at least two weeks before your visit. Bedecked with murals by James Auchiah (Kiowa), Woody Crumbo (Potawatomi), Velino Herrera (Zia Pueblo), Allan Houser (Warm Springs Chiricahua Apache), Stephen Mopope (Kiowa), and Gerald Nailor (Navajo), the DOI building features a great many Indian motifs throughout. One gallery of the DOI's museum is devoted to Indian culture and artifacts, and the wonderful Indian Craft Shop represents artists from 45 tribal areas across the U.S., with a range of goods that includes ceramics, weaving, jewelry, basketry, sculpture, and traditional Alaska Native artwork. The shop, open without an appointment, also boasts an outdoor sculpture garden.

On display at the **Library of Congress** is an exhibition entitled *Exploring the Americas*, which examines the history of the Americas from the pre-European contact period to the conquest and aftermath. Learn about how drastically and irrevocably the world changed through rare maps, documents, prints, paintings, and artifacts of the period.

Washington is also a final resting place for a number of Native people. Several tribal delegates who died during visits to D.C. are buried at **Congressional Cemetery** (1801 E Street, SE; 202-543-0539); **www.congressionalcemetery.org,** and Indian veterans from the Spanish-American War, World Wars I and II, the Korean War, Vietnam, and the Gulf Wars are interred at the **Arlington National Cemetery** (Memorial Drive, Arlington, Virginia; 703-607-8000); **www.arlingtoncemetery.mil**. Located at Arlington Cemetery next to the grave of Lt. Col. Carl Thorpe (Sac and Fox/Pawnee, d. 1986), the son of athlete Jim Thorpe, is the "Grandfather Plaque," a headstone-sized monument honoring Native American veterans. The plaque is the site of a pipe ceremony every Veterans' Day.

—Mitchell Bush (Onondaga), President Emeritus, American Indian Society

2
LEVEL

The Roanoke Museum Store features jewelry, textiles, and other works by Native artisans.

- *Return to a Native Place*
  Algonquian Peoples of the
  Chesapeake **exhibition**

- **Roanoke Museum Store**

- **Sealaska Gallery**

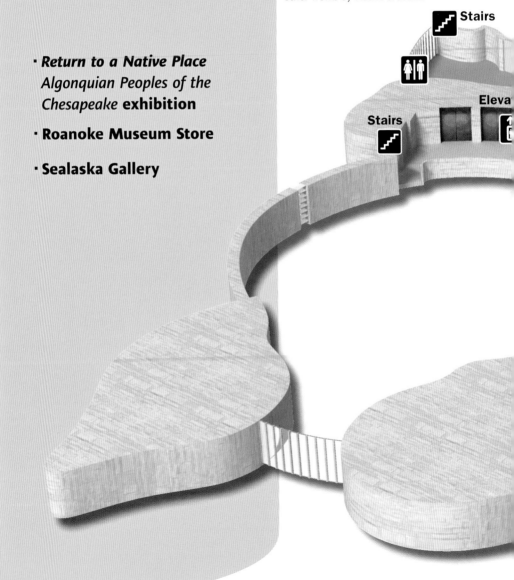

Stairs

Stairs

Eleva

Meet the Native peoples of the Chesapeake Bay region—what is now Washington, D.C., Maryland, Virginia, and Delaware—through photographs, maps, ceremonial and everyday objects, and interactives.

The *Mitsitam Cafe Cookbook* is available in the Roanoke Museum Store.

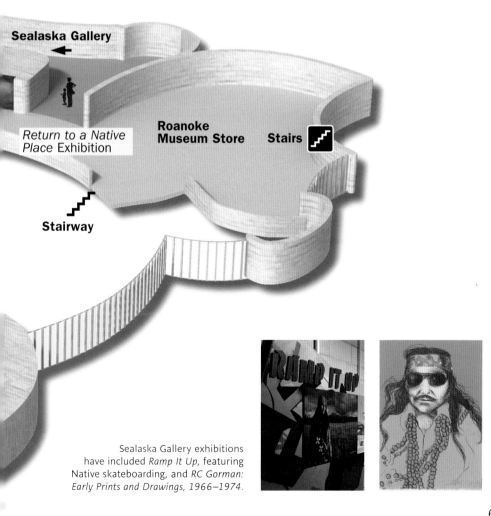

Sealaska Gallery exhibitions have included *Ramp It Up*, featuring Native skateboarding, and *RC Gorman: Early Prints and Drawings, 1966–1974*.

EXTENDED CAPTIONS

p. 22: (Top, l-r:) Ta Dah (Father), Gia (Mother), and Hin Chae (Little One); (middle) Po Khwee (Moon Woman), sculptures of the *Always Becoming* series by artist Nora Naranjo-Morse (Santa Clara Pueblo), 2007.

p. 31: (Clockwise, from top left) The Cachimuel family (Quechua) performs contemporary Andean dance and music; Juanita Velasco (Ixil Maya) demonstrates cooking techniques during NMAI's celebration of Aval, a Mayan Corn Planting Celebration from the highlands of Guatemala; the Rawhide Singers (Blackfeet) perform northern traditional dances and grass dances; and the Wa:k Tab Basket Dancers (Tohono O'odham).

p. 41: (Clockwise, from top left) Dance festival in the Qasgiq, John McIntyre (left) and Joe Chief, Jr., from Bethel, Alaska; Qualla Boundary, homelands of the Eastern Band of Cherokee, North Carolina; Children in the town of Santa María, Huatulco, Mexico, celebrating Quatro Viernes (the fourth Friday of Lent); Prickly pear and saguaro cacti in the homelands of the Tohono O'odham, Arizona.

p. 43: Rick Bartow (Mad River Wiyot, b. 1946), *Bear Mask*, 1990. Wood, paint, metal, horsehair, cotton cloth, glass beads, shells, animal bone, raffia, 37 x 46 x 22 cm. 25/4798

p. 55: (top) James Lavadour (Walla Walla), *Blanket*, 2005. Oil on board, 183 x 396 x 5 cm. 26/6079; (bottom, left) Jim Yellowhawk (Minneconjou Lakota, b. 1958), Lakota Horse Mask, 2008. Paper, acrylic paint, gold leaf, 80.5 x 56.7 x 101.8 cm. 26/7199; (bottom, right) Parade bags, 2009. Made by Jackie Larson Bread (Pikuni, b. 1960). Deerhide, glass beads, rawhide, nylon thread, 27.5 x 28 x 3.5 cm. 26/7250

p. 63: R.C. Gorman (Navajo, 1931–2005), *Self Portrait*, 1973. Lithograph print on paper, 24.3 x 33 cm. 25/9364

PHOTO CREDITS

Images from the photo archives of the National Museum of the American Indian (NMAI) are identified by photograph or negative number where they appear. Individual NMAI staff photographers are listed by name: Ernest Amoroso, Katherine Fogden, Cynthia Frankenburg, Alexandra Harris, Walter Larrimore, Hayes Lavis, and R.A. Whiteside.

Cover, Judy Davis/Hoachlander Davis Photography, © 2004; back cover, R.A. Whiteside; Flap, Wood Ronsaville Harlin, Inc.; 1, John Harrington and Smithsonian Institution, © 2004; 2–3, © Maxwell MacKenzie; 5, (top), Chris Wood/ Smith Group (middle), Cynthia Frankenburg, (bottom), Ernest Amoroso; 6, Guarina Lopez-Davis (Pascua Yaqui); 8–9, Wood Ronsaville Harlin, Inc.; 10, Frank G. Speck; 11, Richard Strauss, © Smithsonian Institution; 13, Guarina Lopez-Davis (Pascua Yaqui); 14, Ernest Amoroso; 17, (top) Felipe Gonzales, (middle) R.A. Whiteside, (bottom) Justin Estoque; 18, © Maxwell MacKenzie; 19, © Maxwell MacKenzie, except top, left © Robert C. Lautman; 20–21, digital illustrations by Lou Spirito; 22, (top and middle) Ernest Amoroso, (bottom) Hayes P. Lavis; 23, (top) Hayes P. Lavis, (middle) Hayes P. Lavis, (bottom) Katherine Fogden (Mohawk); 24, (top) R.A. Whiteside, (bottom) Kerrick James/Getty Images; 25, © Maxwell MacKenzie; 26, (top), R.A. Whiteside, (bottom) © Maxwell MacKenzie; 27, all photos © Maxwell MacKenzie; 28, Claudio Miranda, © Smithsonian Institution; 29, (top left) Walter Larrimore, (top right) © Renée Comet Photography, Inc., Restaurant Associates, and Smithsonian Institution, (bottom) R.A. Whiteside; 30, Cynthia Frankenburg; 31, all by Katherine Fogden (Mohawk) except lower right by R.A. Whiteside; 32, (left) Chris Wood/Smith Group, (right) © Maxwell MacKenzie; 33, top and bottom left by Katherine Fogden (Mohawk), top right by R.A. Whiteside, bottom right by Ernest Amoroso; 34 (top left) Cynthia Frankenburg, (top right) Edward H. Davis, (both middle and bottom) Walter Larrimore; 35, (left) Ernest Amoroso, (right) Katherine Fogden (Mohawk); 36, all photos by Katherine Fogden (Mohawk); 37, (top) © Maxwell MacKenzie, (bottom left) Claudio Miranda, © Smithsonian Institution, (bottom right) Katherine Fogden (Mohawk); 38 and 39, (left, all) © Renée Comet Photography, Inc., Restaurant Associates, and Smithsonian Institution, (right) © Maxwell MacKenzie; 40, Ernest Amoroso; 41, (top left) © James Barker, (top right) R.A. Whiteside, (bottom left) R.A. Whiteside, (bottom right) © Roberto Ysáis; 42, © Maxwell MacKenzie; 43, (top left) Ernest Amoroso, (top right) Walter Larrimore, (bottom), Ernest Amoroso; 44, stills from the Lelawi Theater presentation *Who We Are*; 45, © Maxwell MacKenzie; 46, Walter Larrimore; 47, (top) Walter Larrimore, (middle and bottom) Ernest Amoroso; 48, Walter Larrimore; 49, (top row, l-r) Walter Larrimore, Ernest Amoroso, (middle row, l-r), Walter Larrimore, Katherine Fogden, (bottom), Walter Larrimore; 50, Walter Larrimore; 51, NMAI Photo Services; 52, (top) Walter Larrimore, (bottom left) Walter Larrimore, (bottom right) Ernest Amoroso; 53, (bottom left) Walter Larrimore, (bottom right) R.A. Whiteside; 54, Walter Larrimore; 55 (top left) R.A. Whiteside, (top right) Ernest Amoroso, (bottom, both) Ernest Amoroso; 56, Walter Larrimore; 57, Walter Larrimore; 58, Walter Larrimore; 59, (top) Ernest Amoroso, (bottom), Ernest Amoroso; 60, (both) Alexandra Harris (Cherokee); 62, Alexandra Harris (Cherokee); 63, (top left) Frank G. Speck, (bottom left) Katherine Fogden (Mohawk), (bottom right) Ernest Amoroso.